Grammar

John Butterworth

Illustrations by Lee Nicholls

OXFORD
UNIVERSITY PRESS

UNIVERSITY PRESS

Great Clarendon Street, Oxford OX2 6DP

Oxford University Press is a department of the University of Oxford.
It furthers the University's objective of excellence in research, scholarship,
and education by publishing worldwide in

Oxford New York

Athens Auckland Bangkok Bogotá Buenos Aires Calcutta
Cape Town Chennai Dar es Salaam Delhi Florence Hong Kong Istanbul
Karachi Kuala Lumpur Madrid Melbourne Mexico City Mumbai
Nairobi Paris São Paulo Singapore Taipei Tokyo Toronto Warsaw

with associated companies in Berlin Ibadan

Oxford is a registered trade mark of Oxford University Press
in the UK and in certain other countries

British Library Cataloguing in Publication Data available

ISBN 0–19–910549–9

1 3 5 7 9 10 8 6 4 2

Designed and Typeset by Mike Brain Graphic Design Limited
Printed in China

Contents

Tim and Lucy

Simon the Spyman

Harold the Hiker

Grump – the Beast of Muddyfield Farm

Sentences how words make sense

Sentences do things with words.

They can *say* things; they can *ask* things; they can *tell* people to do things:

Meet Simon.
Who's Simon?
Simon is a spy.
Rubbish!

These are all sentences.

This is a sentence.   So is this.

There are four main kinds of sentence:

statements   commands
questions   exclamations

Statements
are for giving information or telling stories.

> Chapter One
>
> Simon was a spy. His job was to find out secrets and pass them to other spies. He wrote messages in code and hid them in strange places. Once he hid all his papers inside an old football. They would be safe there, he thought. But that's where he was wrong . . .

The sentences in this bit of story are all statements.

Commands
tell you what to do.

Have a nice day.

Meet Simon.

Keep off the grass.

Stop!

Take care.

Give me that!

Questions ask things

Many questions begin with:

who   what   which   when   where   why

You can call these **Wh- questions**.

<u>Who</u> is that man?
<u>What</u>'s he doing?
<u>Why</u> is he hiding?

There is another kind of question that asks if something is so or not.

Is he still there?
Can you see him?
Do you think he's a spy?

Questions like these are called **Yes/No** questions.
Why do you think they are called that?

Full sentences – and others
Often you don't need to use full sentences, especially for speaking.

What would these speakers have said if they had used full sentences?

 'Scared?'

 'Who, me?'

 'Yeah, you.'

 'Course not.'

Exclamations have feeling!

An exclamation is a sentence said with feeling, like surprise or amusement.

What a funny looking man!
How stupid he looks!

Exclamations often begin with *How . . .* or *What . . .* and in writing they always end with an exclamation mark.

Words: players in a team

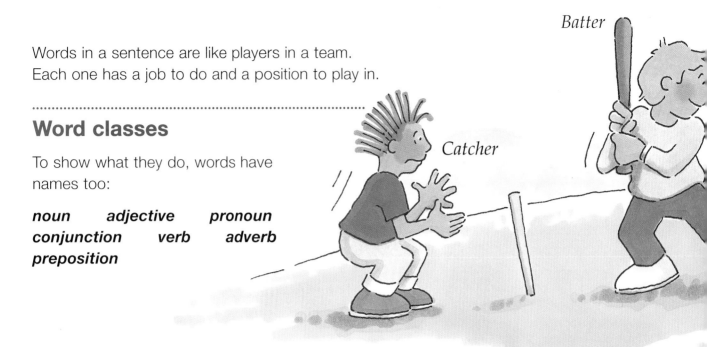

Batter

Catcher

Words in a sentence are like players in a team.
Each one has a job to do and a position to play in.

Word classes

To show what they do, words have
names too:

**noun   adjective   pronoun
conjunction   verb   adverb
preposition**

The names are called **word classes**
You can find them next to the headwords in your
dictionary:

Spectator

throw *verb* (throws, throwing, threw, thrown)
   send something through the air
ball *noun* (balls)
   a round object used in many games

Word classes are also called **Parts of Speech**

In sentences words have jobs and positions, like the players do:

| noun | | adverb |

The   next   batter   whacked   the   ball   high   into   the   air.

| adjective | verb | noun | preposition | noun |

There are players who can play in more than one position, and there are
words that can be in more than one class. For example, 'whack':

Lucy can really <u>whack</u> the ball   or   *She gave the ball a real <u>whack</u>*

| verb | | noun |

Word class depends on the job a word does and where it goes in the sentence.

Fielder

Bowler

Short leg

Word forms

Many words have to change to suit different sentences:

One *player chases* the ball.
Both *players chase* the ball.
Lucy *chased* the ball.
Tim was *chasing* it too.

player and *players* are different forms of the same word.
So are *chase, chases, chased* and *chasing*.

Look on page 6 and find all the forms of the verb *throw*

Look in a dictionary and find all the forms of the verbs: *catch   drop   run*

Phrases
A phrase is a string of words that makes sense but isn't a full sentence.

right out of the park   *whacked the ball*   *Tim's sister*

Put these three **phrases** together to make a full sentence.

Nouns people, animals, things, and stuff

Meet Grump. Grump is a bull.

bull is a noun.

Nouns are words for things, including living things:

bull   gate   farm   hiker   mud

These words are called common nouns.

Grump is a noun too. It's the <u>name</u> of a particular bull.

Grump   Harold   Muddyfield Farm

Names are called *proper nouns*.

....

One – or more?

bull is a **singular noun** – it means there's just one. But most nouns have a **plural form**, for two things or more.

Singular Form	Plural Form
bull	*bulls*
gate	*gates*
hiker	*hikers*

Adding *-s* is the **regular** way to make a noun plural.
'Regular' means the most usual.

But there are also many nouns with ***irregular*** plurals:

goose   geese   hoof   hooves
mouse   mice   sheep   sheep

Uncountable

Counting is fine for things and people, but not for stuff, like

grass   mud   butter   bread

Can you see why nouns like this are called 'uncountable'?
Try saying

one mud,   two muds,   three muds . . . !

Invisible

Bulls and *gates* and *hikers* and *mud* are solid things you can see or touch.

But there are some things you can't see or touch:

danger   fear   stupidity   speed   luck   fun

We call these words **abstract nouns**.

Can you think of any more abstract nouns?

Collective nouns

are words for groups or sets of things:

a party of hikers   a herd of cattle
a crowd of spectators   a flock of sheep

Collective nouns have plural forms too:

herds of cattle   flocks of sheep

English has some peculiar collective nouns.
Did you know that a collection of geese is often called a *gaggle*?

See what other unusual collective nouns you can find.

Always plural

There are English nouns with no singular form. Here are some of them:

scissors   trousers   cattle   gymnastics

Noun phrases describing things

bull is a word – a **noun**
the old bull is a phrase – a **noun phrase**

Noun phrases have the same sort of meanings as nouns – people, animals, things, and stuff. Here are some more noun phrases:

Which is the noun in each of these phrases?

the old brown bull
a muddy field
tired hikers
great danger
a wooden gate

> **A noun phrase nearly always has a noun in it, and the noun is the main word in the phrase.**

Building noun phrases

As you can see, you need more than just nouns to build noun phrases:

old   muddy   tired   great   wooden

are describing words for using with nouns. They belong to a big class of words called **adjectives**, (see pages 12–13).

Starters

At the beginning of noun phrases the most common words are   *the   a   an*
But here are some more very useful noun phrase starters.

this   that   these   those   all   some   any   no   every   each
either   neither   several   enough   such   many   much   more
most   few   little   my   your   her   his   our   their

All these words are special kinds of adjectives.
Try making up some noun phrases that start with them.

Possessive nouns

Harold's backpack
This phrase shows that the backpack belongs to Harold.

Harold's is called the **possessive form** of the noun *Harold*.
(A *possession* is a belonging.)

Notice that the possessive noun is spelt with
the sign **'** which is called an **apostrophe**.

Common nouns also have a possessive form.

*the **bull's** horns*	*the **farmer's** field*
*the **tree's** leaves*	***Grump's** nasty temper*

An apostrophe means that something has been left out of a word.
A long time ago, possessive nouns in English ended in *-es*:

the mannes hat   the dogges bone

Gradually the *e* disappeared, but the apostrophe stayed, to
show where the *e* once was. One day the apostrophe may
disappear, too. Language is always changing.

If the owner is plural,
and ends in an *-s* the
apostrophe goes after
the *s*.

the bulls' horns
the hikers' packs

Adjectives working with nouns

The man in the hat could be **either** of these:

The short man in the floppy hat could only be **one** of them.

It's the adjectives *short* and *floppy* that make the difference:

Adjectives work with nouns, describing people and things.

Which noun does *short* work with?
Which noun does *floppy* work with?

Adjectives give many different sorts of information about nouns.
Here are some sorts, with examples of the adjectives:

	Adjectives				
SIZE	*large*	*long . . .*			
SHAPE	*round*	*floppy . . .*			
COLOUR	*brown*	*red . . .*			
FEEL	*hard*	*smooth*	*cold*	*wet . . .*	
NATURE	*bad*	*strange*	*suspicious*	*dangerous*	*secret . . .*
AGE	*new*	*young*	*old*	*ancient . . .*	
NUMBER	*twelve*	*twenty*	*first*	*last*	*next . . .*

Adjectives can be used in front of nouns to make **noun phrases**:

a suspicious parcel   *secret documents*
a wet, chilly afternoon   *a bright, warm, spring morning*

Most adjectives – but not all – can also be used to finish off sentences:

The parcel looked suspicious.
            The documents were highly secret.
                        The afternoon was wet and chilly.

Making the difference

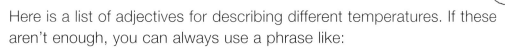

cold   chilly   cool   mild   warm   hot

Here is a list of adjectives for describing different temperatures. If these aren't enough, you can always use a phrase like:

very hot   *terribly cold*   *quite warm*   *really windy*

Think of an adjective or phrase that describes the weather where you are today.

Words like *very, terribly, quite, really* etc., are called *adverbs*.
You can find out about adverbs on page 20.

More and Most

Many adjectives have forms that can be used to *compare* things. They are called the **comparative** and **superlative**:

	Comparative	**Superlative**
a warm day	*a warmer day*	*the warmest day this year*

The regular forms are made by just adding *-er* and *-est* to the adjective.
But some adjectives are *irregular*:

Adjective	**Comparative**	**Superlative**
heavy	*heavier*	*heaviest*
far	*further*	*furthest*
good	*better*	*best*
bad	*worse*	*worst*

Not all adjectives have their own forms for comparing. You have to make them into phrases using *more* or *most*:

Comparative	**Superlative**
more difficult	*the most difficult*
more dangerous	*the most dangerous*

Pronouns words for nouns

Pronouns are words for people, animals, and things – just like nouns.

These pronouns are called **personal pronouns**.

Some pronouns are for *female* things only   *she   her*
Some are for *male* things only   *he   him*

Pronouns by themselves are *blank*. They can mean almost anything. So when you use a pronoun you must make it clear what, or who, it does mean.

SECRETS OF THE PARK BENCH

When Tim and Lucy Boswell found an old football under a bench in the park, **they** had no idea **it** belonged to Simon the Spyman, or that hidden inside were secret papers. Simon was so desperate to get **them** back, that **he** followed the two children.

What do the four pronouns in this story mean?

Person

person has a special meaning in grammar. There are three 'persons' – the first is for *me* (or *us*), the second is for *you* and the third is for *everyone*, and *everything*, else.

Personal Pronouns	Singular	Plural
1ST PERSON	*I me*	*we us*
2ND PERSON	*you*	*you*
3RD PERSON	*he him*	*they*
	she her it	*them*

There are **singular** 'persons' and **plural** 'persons'.
But what do you notice about the pronoun *you*?

Each of these sentences is written in a different 'person'. Which is which?

Did *you* know *you* were carrying secret documents?
I noticed *we* were being followed by a strange-looking man.
They threw away the ball, and ran for it.

Possessive pronouns

are for talking about things which belong to someone.

my   your   his   her
its   our   their
mine   yours   hers
ours   theirs

Spell check: There are no apostrophes in possessive pronouns.

Some possessive pronouns are like adjectives:

<u>*my*</u> *brother*   <u>*his*</u> *football*
<u>*their*</u> *secrets*

Some are like nouns:

That's not <u>yours</u>, it's <u>mine</u>!

More pronouns

who   whom   what   which   whose

someone and *something* are pronouns too. So are:

anyone   everyone   no one
anything   everything   nothing

These pronouns are for asking questions.

Verbs doing, being, and having

Most verbs are about *doing* certain things, but there are verbs about *being* and *having* certain things, as well.

*Grump **lives** alone in a field. He **has** a very bad temper. When he **is** angry he **bellows**, and **stamps** his feet. He **charges** about, **breaking** fences and **throwing** hikers into hedges. Grump really **hates** hikers.*

Doing words

live, bellow, stamp, charge, break, throw and *hate* are all verbs. They are words that tell us what things or people <u>do</u>.

Verb forms

Verbs can change their form to fit different sentences. Most verbs have four or five different forms. You can find out what these are from your dictionary. For example:

bellow *verb* **bellows, bellowing, bellowed**

The usual way to change the form of a verb is to add *-s, -ed* or *-ing*.

Some verbs have an extra form that usually ends in *-en*:

break *verb* **breaks, breaking, broke, broken**
fall *verb* **falls, falling, fell, fallen**

-s, -ing, -ed, -en are the **regular** verb endings.
But some verb forms are **irregular**. For example:

threw (not **throwed**)   *broke* (not **breaked**)   *thrown* (not **throwen**)

Verbs have more forms than any other English words, but not nearly as many as some languages. The French verb **jeter**, which means **throw**, has about 30 forms including:

jeter jeté jetes jetons jetez jettent jetai jetais jetterai . . .

And some languages have hundreds! (Think yourself lucky.)

be and have

Two of the most important verbs in English are *have* and *be*, and all their different forms.

*He **has** a bad temper*   *He **is** very angry.*

They are very irregular, especially *be*:

be *verb* **am   are   is   being   was   were   been**
have *verb* **has   having   had**

··

Auxiliary Verbs – the helpers

Often verbs work together in teams, with a **main verb** and one or more *helper verbs* – called *auxiliaries* – in front of it. This makes a **verb phrase**:

The three hikers <u>had been walking</u> all day.
Grump <u>was bellowing</u> at the top of his voice.

  had, been, and *was* are the helper verbs.
  walking and *bellowing* are the main verbs.

Some more **auxiliary verbs** are:

can   could   will   shall   would   should   may   might

Bulls <u>can move</u> very quickly for such large animals.
Harold <u>should have stayed</u> on his side of the gate.
He <u>might have been hurt</u> very badly.

Another busy auxiliary verb is *do*, with its forms *does, doing, did, done*:

Grump really <u>does hate</u> hikers.
Poor Harold <u>didn't have</u> a chance.

Tense past, present, future

Tense is about *time*: past, present, and future.

The past tense

is for saying what *happened*, or how things *were*. It is the usual tense for stories.

Simon called his boss and told him he had hidden the secret documents inside an old football under the park bench. But when he put down the phone, the football had gone.

The present tense

is for describing things, for writing stage or film directions and giving commentaries.

Simon is a spy, but not a very good one. Everyone knows he's a spy. He wears sunglasses and a long overcoat, which are a complete giveaway. And he loses things all the time.

'Tim has the ball in front of the goal. He shoots – and scores! Ye-es!'

The future tense

is for saying what will happen, or may happen.

"Simon's boss will be furious when he finds out. He might even give him the sack. Simon won't be using that hiding place again. Silly man!"

The future is the tense for giving *forecasts* and *predictions*:

Tomorrow will be wet and windy.

Simple tenses

English verbs, on their own, can only show two tenses – present and past. These are called **simple tenses**:

Verb	Call	Tell	Hide
PRESENT	call or calls	tell or tells	hide or hides
PAST	called	told	hid

Which of these has a *regular* past tense? Which are *irregular*?

Why do you think there are two forms to choose from for the present tense?
(You can find out on page 24–25.)

Other tenses

There are other ways of making tenses with the help of auxiliary verbs like:

is   was   will   have   were . . .

For example:

PRESENT	*is calling*	*am telling*	*are hiding*
PAST	*was calling*	*was telling*	*were hiding*
	has called	*have told*	*have hidden*
	had called	*had told*	*had hidden*
FUTURE	*will call*	*will tell*	*will hide*

Don't mix tenses!

Be careful – especially when you are writing – not to change from one tense to another in mid sentence. It is easy to do, but it's confusing for the reader.

He puts down the phone and saw that the ball has gone.

This sentence is a mess! Which two tenses have been *mixed*? How would you put the sentence right?

Adverbs working with verbs

Adverbs can be used to say *how*, *when*, or *where* something happens:

loudly   angrily   yesterday   now   here   there

Grump snorted angrily.   **How?** *Angrily.*
The hikers should be arriving soon.   **When?** *Soon.*
A large brown bull lives here.   **Where?** *Here.*

A lot of English adverbs are formed by adding *-ly* to the end of an adjective.

ADJECTIVE   loud   angry   bad
ADVERB   loudly   angrily   badly

But not all adverbs end in *-ly*. These are adverbs too:

soon   fast   together   afterwards   home . . .

In most sentences adverbs work with verbs and add to their meaning:

Adverbs are real wanderers. You can find them almost anywhere in a sentence.

Suddenly there was a loud roar.
Grump snorted crossly and lowered his horns menacingly.
Harold was soon running frantically towards the gate.

Some adverbs can be used with adjectives – or with other adverbs – to alter their meaning.

more   most   very   extremely   dreadfully   horribly
absolutely   less   quite   fairly   rather   slightly   so   not . . .

Here are some phrases with these adverbs in:

<u>*absolutely*</u> *furious*   *a <u>very</u> loud roar*   <u>*horribly*</u> *sharp horns*
<u>*rather*</u> *crossly*   <u>*less*</u> *friendly*   <u>*quite*</u> *soon*

What difference do these adverbs make?

Prepositions and conjunctions

Prepositions are small words but they are very busy ones. Most of them are to do with the *position* things are in or the *direction* they're going.

in on under over by from to with beside through between up across into at with of . . .

They are used in front of nouns, or noun phrases, or even pronouns, to make short phrases like:

across some fields   *through mud*   *over the gate*

Conjunctions link up words and phrases and sentences. The conjunctions that are used most are *and, or* and *but*:

Harold and Jamila
a short cut across the field or a long walk round
The animal looked friendly but it was mean and bad-tempered.

Here are some more conjunctions:

although because before for if so since unless until when whether while . . .

What's in a sentence? the main parts

Most *full* sentences have a **subject** and a **verb**. Some also have an **object** or **complement**.

Subject

The **subject** of a sentence is *who* or *what* the sentence is about.

Lucy won the race.
In this sentence *Lucy* is the subject. She won the race.

The green car came last.
In this sentence *the green car* is the subject. It came last.

It got a puncture in the front tyre.
In this sentence *it* is the subject. *It* got the puncture.

The subject of a sentence can be:
a **noun** (like *Lucy*)   a **noun phrase** (like *the green car*)
or a **pronoun** (like *it*)

The subject can be singular or plural:

The other cars were a long way behind.

What is the subject of this sentence? Is it singular or plural?

Predicate

The rest of a sentence, without the subject, is called the **predicate**.
The predicate is the part of the sentence that has the verb in.

. . . won the race.   . . . came last.
. . . were a long way behind.

The predicate can be a verb on its own:

. . . swerved.   . . . stopped.   . . . lost.

Think of some different subjects you could give to these predicates.

Verb

Every *full* sentence of English has a **verb**.
The verb in a sentence is like the engine in a car.

The verb may finish the sentence by itself:
Lucy won.

Or it may be followed by other words
or phrases:
Lucy was the winner.

The Verb in a sentence,
means the whole verb, including any helpers:

*The green car **would have won**, but for the puncture.*

Object

Sometimes the verb has an **object** as well as a subject:

*Lucy beat **Tim**.*   *Tim's car hit the **cones**.*

The object is who or what something happens to, like being *beaten* or getting *hit*.

Complement

In some sentences the verb is followed by a description of the subject:

*Tim looks **angry**.*   *Lucy is the **champion**.*

This part is called the **complement**. The complement says what the subject *is*, or what the subject is like.

Agreement verbs and subjects

In English – and in many other languages – the verb may change its form to suit different subjects. This is called **agreeing**.

The verb that changes most is the verb *to be*. These are the changes it makes:

Other verbs hardly change at all.

Subject	Present Tense	Past Tense	Singular	Present Tense	Past Tense
I	*am*	*was*	1ST PERSON	*like*	*liked*
you	*are*	*were*	2ND PERSON	*like*	*liked*
he, she, it	*is*	*was*	3RD PERSON	*likes*	*liked*
			Plural		
we	*are*	*were*	1ST PERSON	*like*	*liked*
you	*are*	*were*	2ND PERSON	*like*	*liked*
they	*are*	*were*	3RD PERSON	*like*	*liked*

See how agreement works in sentences:

I <u>am</u> your friend.   *You <u>were</u> my friend.*   *She <u>is</u> our friend.*

I <u>like</u> pizza.   *He <u>likes</u> kebabs.*   *We <u>like</u> ice-cream.*

If the subject is a noun or a noun phrase, the verb still has to agree:

Tim <u>likes</u> kebabs.
(same as with <u>he</u>)

Lucy and I <u>like</u> ice-cream.
(same as with <u>we</u>)

This spinach <u>is</u> delicious.
(same as with <u>it</u>)

Hot-dogs <u>are</u> disgusting.
(same as with <u>they</u>)

Singular or plural?

These pronouns are singular.

someone	*anyone*	*everyone*	*no one*
something	*anything*	*everything*	*nothing*

That's why you say:

Everyone likes pizza   and   *Nothing beats ice cream*

What verbs would you use if these pronouns were plural?

What about collective nouns? A collective noun, like *team*, is singular, even though there are lots of players in it.
So should you say:

*Our team **is** winning*   OR   *Our team **are** winning?*

The fact is, people say both, and both are all right. Which do you say?

Using pronouns

There are five words in English which can *only* be used as subjects.

They are the personal pronouns: *I   he   she   we   they*
In other parts of the sentence you use: *me   him   her   us   them*

She passed it to me.   *I passed it to them.*

They passed it to us.   *We passed it to him.*   *He dropped it.*

Be careful when you join two pronouns with *and*.

You should say   **He** *and* **I** *are friends*, NOT *Him and me are friends.*

subjects

Building sentences and making changes

The simplest kinds of sentence are short **statements**, like these, with the subject at the beginning and the verb next:

For example:

Lucy won.
The green car hit the cones.
The red car spun off the track.

No it's not!
Adding the word *not* to a statement makes it *negative*.

Lucy has won the race.   *Lucy has not won the race.*
                             has not can be shortened to *hasn't*

The word *not* is placed in the middle of the verb.
So, if the verb is just one word, it may need a helper to make it negative:

Tim won the race.   *Tim did not win the race.*   Which is the
                        did not can be shortened to *didn't*   helper verb?

There are other ways, too, to make a sentence negative:

Nothing has happened yet.   *No one came near.*

I never eat ice cream.   *This room is untidy.*

In English you only need one of these words to make a sentence negative.

For example: *I did**n't** tell him* **nothing**   should be

I told him **nothing**   or   *I did**n't** tell him anything.*

Questions

Remember there are two kinds of question – See page 5.

A Yes/No question is like a statement, but usually with words in a different order. It is the different order of words that turns it into a question:

Statement	**Question**
You have walked a long way	*Have you walked a long way?*
That bull is friendly.	*Is that bull friendly?*
They did have a good time.	*Did they have a good time?*
(They had a good time.)	

Where has the subject moved to in these questions?

Wh- questions nearly always begin with a **Wh-** word – whether it's the subject or not.

<u>What</u> is the matter?   <u>Why</u> are you looking worried?
<u>How</u> did Harold get away?   <u>Who</u> won the race?

What do you think is the subject
in each of these questions?

Commands

Commands often have no subject. The subject is whoever you're speaking to.

Stop!   Enjoy your walk.   Sleep well.

But you can give commands a subject if you want to:

You go away!   Run, Harold!   Everyone stop there!

Which are the subjects of these three commands?

In writing you have punctuation marks to show different kinds of sentence – ?!
In speech you don't. But there are differences you can hear.
Read the sentences on this page and listen for changes in your voice –
especially at the end.

Extra parts phrases and clauses

You can make short sentences longer by adding *phrases* or *clauses*.

Phrases

Let's start with a plain, simple sentence that has no extra parts.

Simon hid the secret documents.

Here it is with an extra phrase added:

Simon hid the secret documents <u>inside an old football</u>.

Extra phrases don't have to be added to the end of a sentence. For example:

<u>For some strange reason</u> Simon hid the secret documents inside an old football.

Clauses

Here is a new sentence.
First you see it on its own,
then with a **clause** added:

Simon left the football under the bench.

Simon left the football under the bench <u>while he made a phone-call</u>.

A clause is another short sentence, with its own subject and verb.
So, in the longer sentence, there are **two** clauses:

Simon left the football under the bench
+ he made a phone call

But instead of being written as two sentences, with a full stop between them, they are joined by the word *while* to make one big sentence.

Clauses and Conjunctions

One way to connect clauses is to use a **conjunction**.
There is a list of conjunctions on page 21.

Here are some conjunctions at work joining clauses:

Simon followed the children home <u>because</u> they had found his football full of secret papers.

Give me that ball <u>or</u> you'll be sorry.

We're not letting you have it <u>unless</u> you say please.

Conjunctions don't have to be in *between* the clauses.
A conjunction can be at the *beginning* of a sentence. Like this:

<u>When</u> *he came out of the phone box, the ball had gone.*

Who, which, that

The pronouns *who, which* and *that* can be used to connect clauses, too, but in a slightly different way:

That's the man <u>who</u> followed us home.

He wants the football <u>that</u> we found under the bench.

Simple or complex?

A **simple** sentence has only one clause.

Give me that ball.	**Simple Sentence**
You'll be sorry.	**Simple Sentence**

A **complex** sentence has two or more clauses joined together.

Give me that ball or you'll be sorry.	**Complex Sentence**

Index

Index

Index